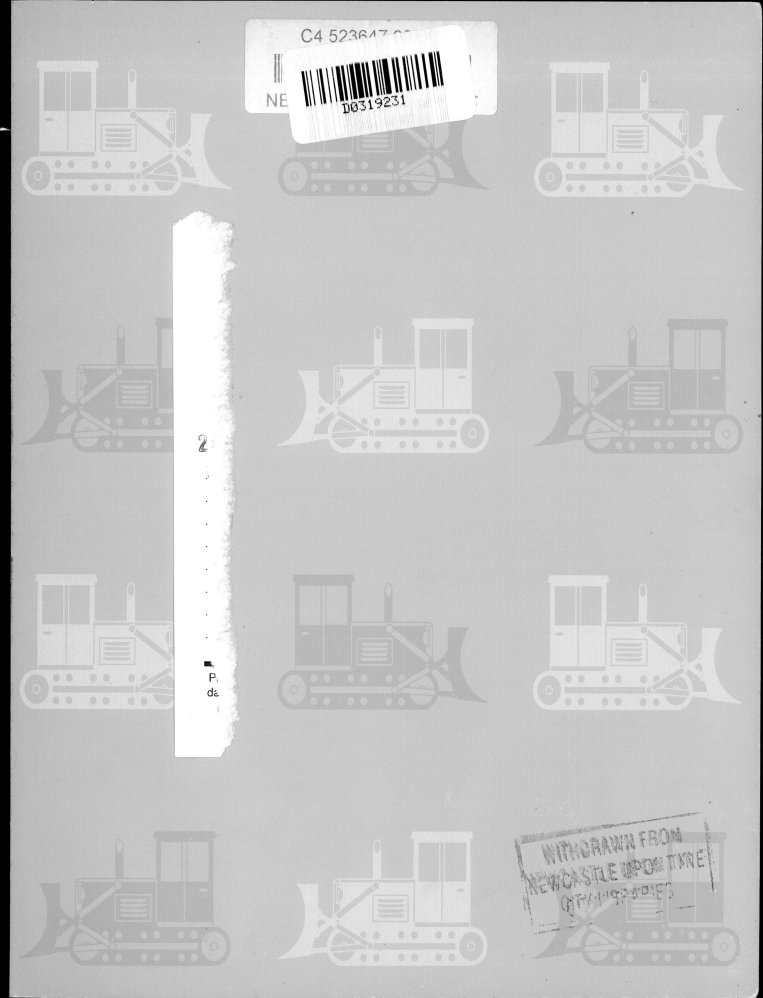

BIG
MACHINES

Bulldozers

David and Penny Glover

FRANKLIN WATTS
LONDON · SYDNEY

This edition 2008

Franklin Watts
338 Euston Road, London, NW1 3BH

Franklin Watts Australia
Level 17/207 Kent Street, Sydney, NSW 2000

Copyright © Franklin Watts 2004

Series editor: Sarah Peutrill
Designer: Richard Langford
Art director: Jonathan Hair
Illustrator: Ian Thompson
Reading consultant: Margaret Perkins, Institute of Education, University of Reading
Picture credits: Jonathan Blair/Corbis: 7t. Digital Vision: 18. Lowell Georgia/Corbis: 21t, 21b.
Courtesy of Komatsu UK: front cover, 4, 8, 12, 23. Courtesy of Komatsu USA: 6, 11t, 13t, 14, 19, 22.
Photri/Topham: 7b. Vittoriano Rastelli/Corbis: 20. Every attempt has been made to clear copyright.
Should there be any inadvertent omission, please apply to the publisher for rectification.

With particular thanks to Komatsu UK and Komatsu USA for permission to use their photographs.

A CIP catalogue record for this book is available from the British Library.

Dewey number: 629.225
ISBN: 978 0 7496 7811 1

Printed in Malaysia

Franklin Watts is a division of Hachette Children's Books, an Hachette Livre UK company.

Contents

At the building site

Bulldozers are big pushing machines. They are sometimes called dozers.

Most bulldozers work on building sites. Their job is to level the ground.

A bulldozer pushes sand into a pile. Another machine, called a digger, will load the pile onto a dumper truck. The truck takes it away.

To bulldoze means to push like a bull. A big bulldozer can push as hard as 100 bulls all at once!

Dozers can do other jobs as well.

This bulldozer is smoothing the sand on a beach.

This bulldozer is knocking down a building.

7

The dozer blade

The dozer's main tool is its giant blade. The blade skims the ground, pushing soil and rocks with tremendous force.

The dozer's blade is made from thick steel so it does not bend or break. The top, bottom and sides are curved to keep the load together as it is pushed along.

Blade

KOMATSU

D 65PX

The driver raises the blade above the ground to drive into position, then lowers it again to push the load.

Hydraulic rams move the blade up and down.

Oil pushes the piston along the cylinder. The force moves the blade.

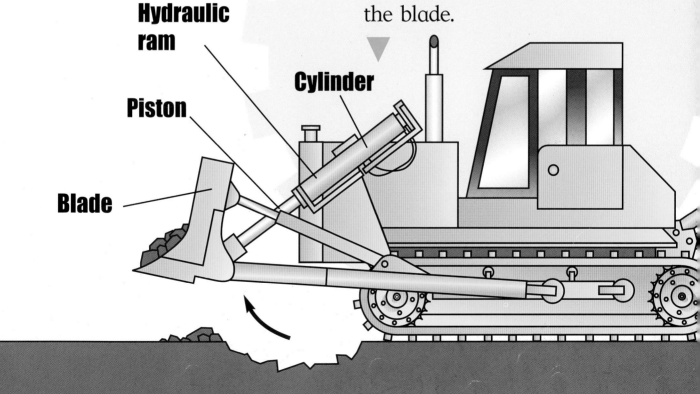

Hydraulic ram

Cylinder

Piston

Blade

The ripper

The bulldozer's blade pushes rocks and soil into piles, but it cannot tear into a hard surface like an old concrete road.
This is a job for the ripper.

The ripper is a big steel finger at the back of the bulldozer.

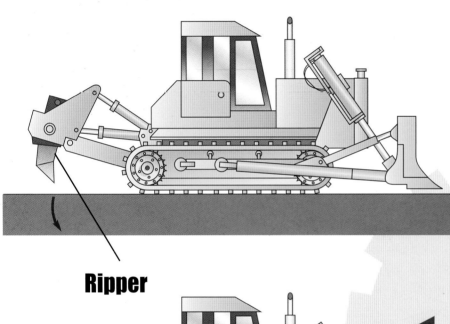

Ripper

The driver lowers the ripper and drives the bulldozer forward. The ripper breaks up the ground, like a fingernail scratching a label off a jar.

Some bulldozers have more than one ripper.

When the ripper has done its work, the driver raises the ripper and lowers the blade to clear the rubble away.

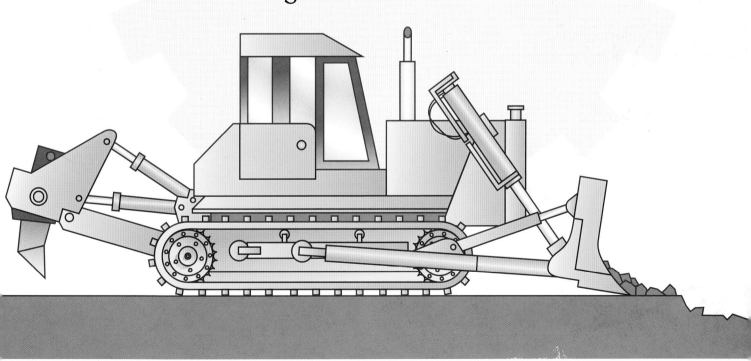

Tracks

Most bulldozers have metal tracks, not wheels. Tracks are loops made from links, like a chain. As the tracks go round, the dozer crawls along.

There are two tracks, one on either side of the machine.

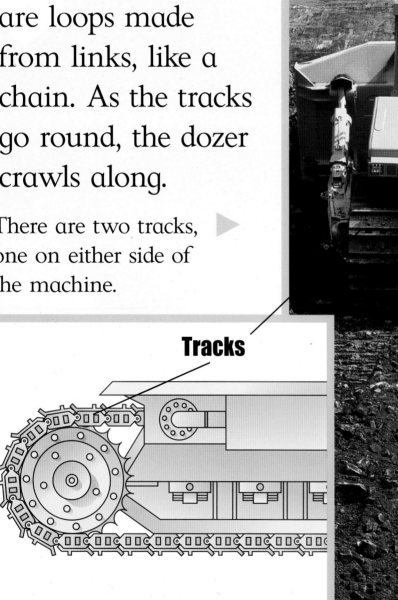

Tracks

Tracks help the bulldozer grip the ground. Wheels with rubber tyres would slip when the bulldozer tried to push hard.

◀ The bulldozer's tracks help it to go over uneven slopes.

Cog

Tracks work like giant bicycle chains. A cog, a wheel with teeth, moves the links around. The cog is turned by the bulldozer's engine.

Link

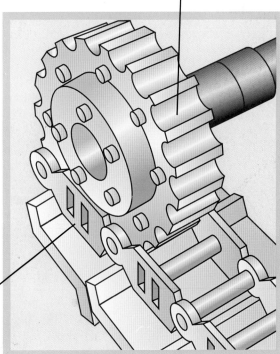

In the cab

The driver sits high up in the cab. Levers and buttons allow the driver to move the different parts.

The bulldozer does not have a steering wheel. Instead the driver steers with levers called joysticks.

Cab

Joystick

The tracks go at different speeds to make the dozer turn left or right, or spin around on the spot.

Straight ahead

Same speed

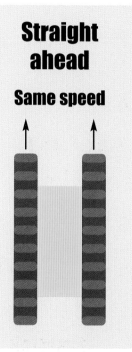

When both tracks move at the same speed the bulldozer goes in a straight line.

Turning left

Slower   Faster

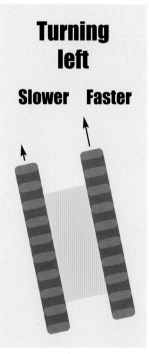

When the right track moves faster than the left, the bulldozer turns left.

Turning right

Faster   Slower

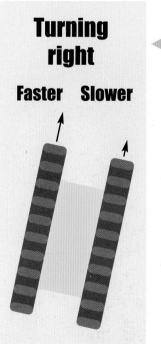

When the left track moves faster than the right, the bulldozer turns right.

Spinning on the spot

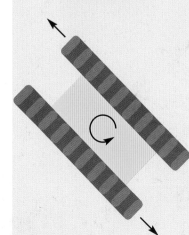

When the tracks move in opposite directions, the bulldozer spins on the spot.

The engine

A bulldozer needs a powerful engine to make it go. The engine runs on diesel fuel. The fuel burns inside the engine, and makes hot gases that push the parts around.

The force in the engine turns gears in the gearbox. Gears carry the force from the engine to the cogs that turn the tracks.

▼

Gearbox

The force goes to the tracks

The engine also turns an oil pump. This pushes oil into the hydraulic rams that move the blade and the ripper.

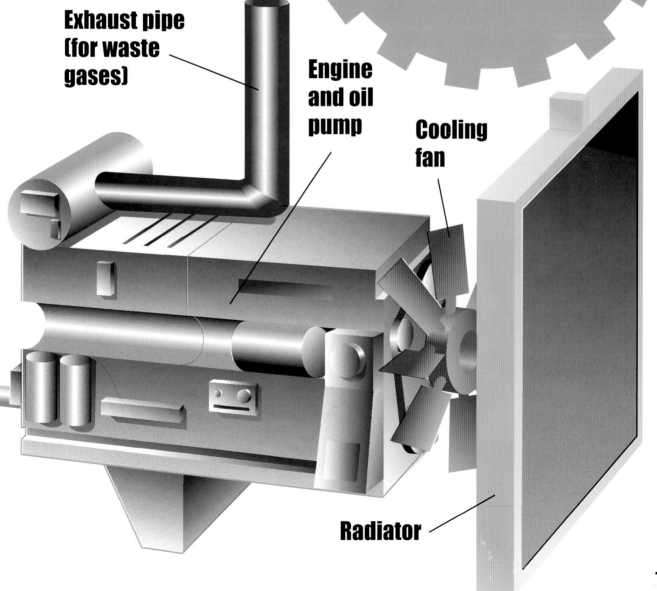

Exhaust pipe (for waste gases)

Engine and oil pump

Cooling fan

Radiator

Hot work

A bulldozer's engine gets very hot as it works.

BIG FACT

A big bulldozer engine produces as much heat as 50 kitchen cookers!

Bulldozers that clear land to make roads have to work hard all day long.

When a car drives fast the wind cools its engine down. But a bulldozer moves slowly, so its heat is not carried away by the breeze.

A giant radiator and fan stop the bulldozer engine from overheating.

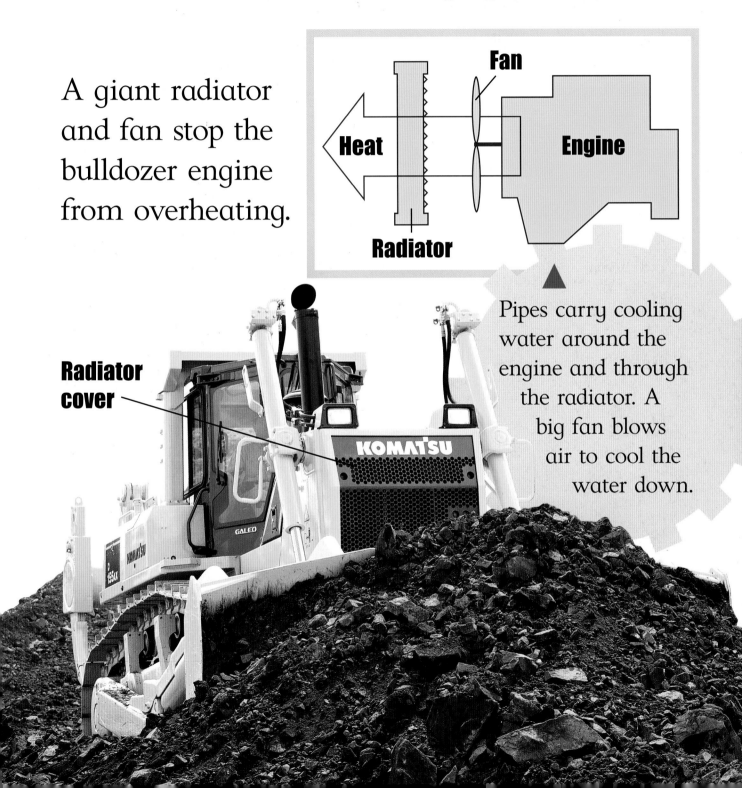

Fan

Heat

Engine

Radiator

Radiator cover

Pipes carry cooling water around the engine and through the radiator. A big fan blows air to cool the water down.

Dozer to the rescue!

A bulldozer's great pushing power
is useful in an emergency.

When a volcano erupts, a bulldozer
can push the lava into banks to
stop it reaching villages and towns.

When snow
blocks a road,
a bulldozer
can clear it.

A bulldozer
pushes sand
and rocks
onto burning
oil to put out
the flames.

A giant bulldozer

The Komatsu D575A is the most powerful bulldozer in the world. It is 11.7 metres long and 4.5 metres tall - that's as big as a house!

▲ The D575A is shown here next to a normal-size bulldozer.

BIG
FACT

The D575A is so big that it must be taken to pieces to travel on ordinary roads. Seven trucks are needed to carry all the parts.

The D575A has a massive blade that can move 180 tonnes of soil or rock at a time.

Make it yourself

Make a model bulldozer.

You will need:

An adult to help

Paints

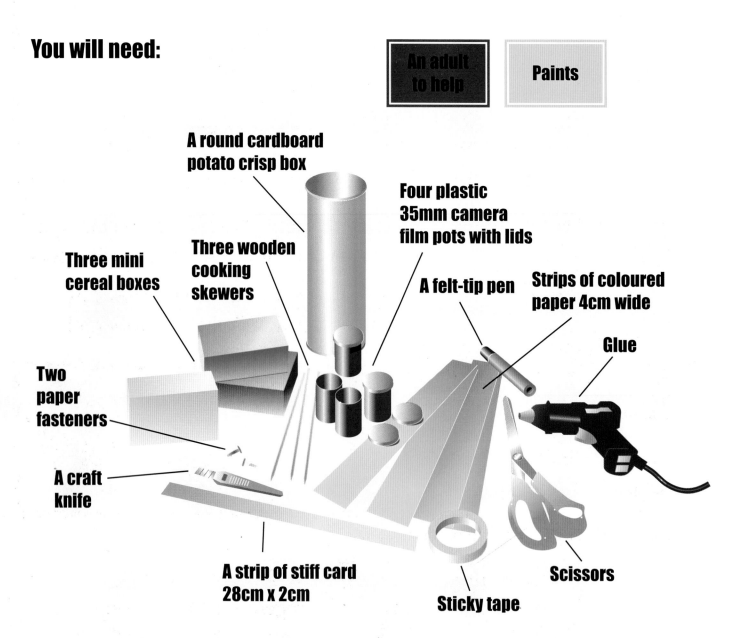

A round cardboard potato crisp box

Four plastic 35mm camera film pots with lids

Three wooden cooking skewers

Three mini cereal boxes

A felt-tip pen

Strips of coloured paper 4cm wide

Glue

Two paper fasteners

A craft knife

A strip of stiff card 28cm x 2cm

Sticky tape

Scissors

SAFETY! An adult must help you with the cutting and sticking.

1. Glue/tape the three boxes together to make the bulldozer body and cab.

Make two pairs of holes on either side of the body. Push a skewer through each pair of holes.

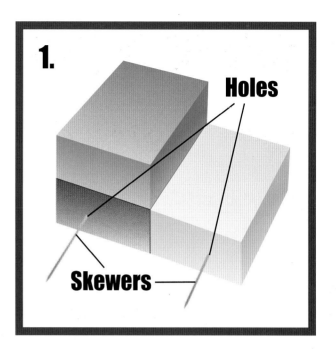

1.

Holes

Skewers

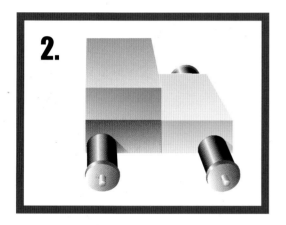

2.

2. Make small holes at the centres of the tops and bottoms of the film pots.

Push the pots onto the skewers as shown. Trim the skewers to length.

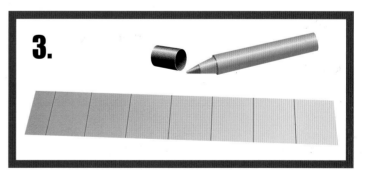

3.

3. Draw lines across the paper strips to mark out links.

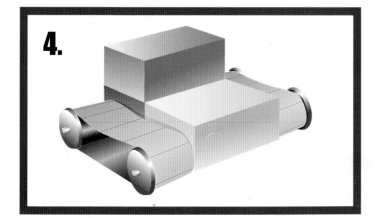

4.

4. Tape the strips together to make loops around the film pots. These are your tracks.

5. Cut the potato crisp box in half along its length. Cut one half so that it is the same width as your bulldozer (including the tracks). This is the blade.

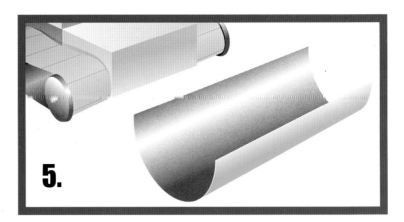

5.

6.

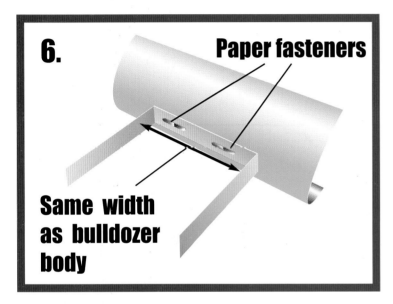

Paper fasteners

Same width as bulldozer body

6. Fold the card strip into a U shape as shown. The width of the U should be the same as the bulldozer's body.

Fix the U to the blade with paper fasteners.

7. Make small holes in the blade's arms and the body. Push a skewer through the holes to attach the blade to the body. Trim the skewer to length.

Use your bulldozer to push a load!

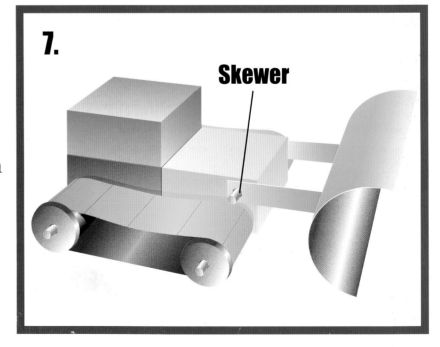

7.

Skewer

Trace your own bulldozer

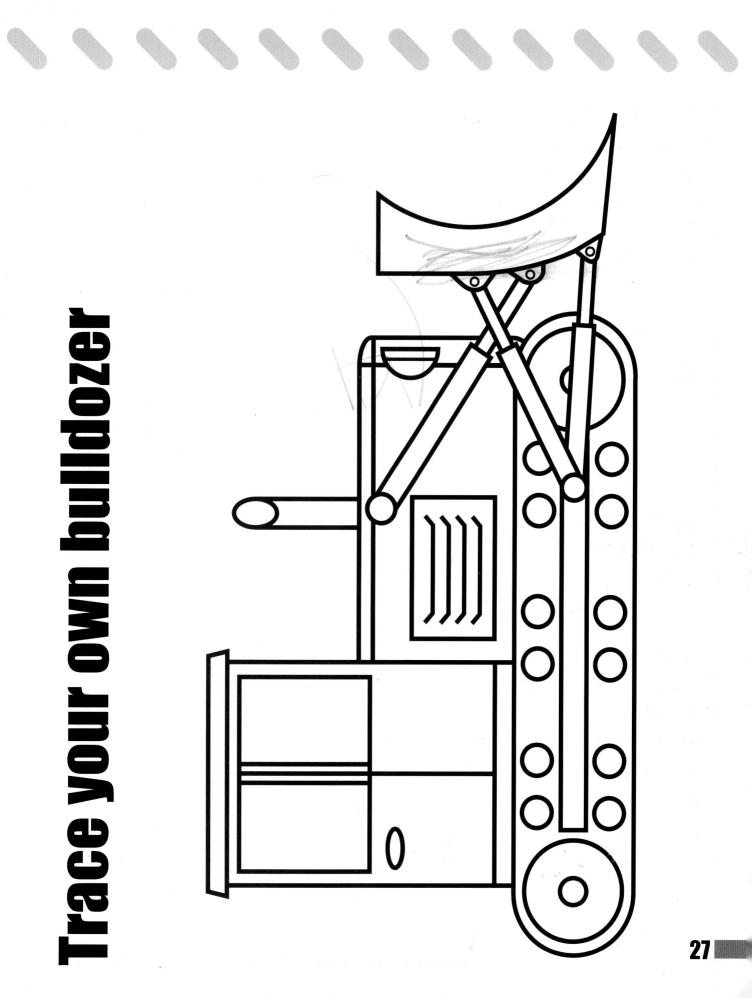

Bulldozer words

blade
The big metal pushing tool at the front of the bulldozer.

cog
A wheel with teeth. Big cogs turn the bulldozer's tracks.

diesel
The fuel the bulldozer engine uses to make it go.

engine
The part of a machine that burns fuel to make the forces that move its parts.

exhaust pipe
Waste gases from the engine go out into the air through this pipe.

hydraulic ram
A part that pushes to move the blade or the ripper. A ram is worked by oil, which pushes a piston along a cylinder.

joystick

A control like a lever for steering the bulldozer.

push

A force that moves objects away from the thing that is pushing. Bulldozers are pushing machines.

radiator

The part that allows heat to escape from the engine. Cooling water goes around the engine and through the radiator. The radiator is cooled by a fan.

ripper

The strong steel spike or finger at the back of a bulldozer. The ripper breaks up hard ground.

steel

A tough, hard metal used to make machines and tools.

track

The loops of metal links that bulldozers have instead of wheels.

Index